The Realness of Witchcraft in America

Witches or no witches, you should read this account!

By
A. Monroe Aurand

First published in 1942

Published by Left of Brain Books

Copyright © 2023 Left of Brain Books

ISBN 978-1-396-32614-1

First Edition

All rights reserved. No part of this publication may be reproduced, distributed, or transmitted in any form or by any means, including photocopying, recording, or other electronic or mechanical methods, without the prior written permission of the publisher, except in the case of brief quotations permitted by copyright law. Left of Brain Books is a division of Left Of Brain Onboarding Pty Ltd.

PUBLISHER'S PREFACE

About the Book

The Realness of Witchcraft in America is a very unique book of Witch Doctors, Pow Wows, Angels, Hex, Apparitions, Hexeru, Devils and Sex. It was written by A. Monroe Aurand Jr. in 1942. What makes a man superstitious, his religion or lack of it? There is witchcraft in America practiced for centuries in unknown places in Pennsylvania. As given by the dictionary, a witch can be anybody man or woman, old or young. Thousands have died or been tortured for this practice since 1233, mostly innocents. Many people throughout the world accept charms as a form of protection from evil. This is an excellent book that explains much of the myths, persecutions, theories and history of this ancient and controversial practice. WITCHES OR NO WITCHES, YOU SHOULD READ THIS ACCOUNT!

CONTENTS

PUBLISHER'S PREFACE
  WHAT MAKES A MAN SUPERSTITIOUS; HIS RELIGION, OR A LACK OF IT? 1
  WITCHCRAFT AND BELIEFS IN EVIL SPIRITS CAME TO AMERICA LONG AGO 5
  PURITANS RAISED HELL WITH WITCHES IN EARLY DAYS.............. 9
  STRANGE EVOLUTION FOR GETTING RID OF EVIL SPIRITS 13
  CHARMS AND TRINKETS ARE REVERED BY MANY OF OUR PEOPLE 17
  SOME OF THE "FAMOUS" WITCH TRIALS IN PENNSYLVANIA..... 20
  THOSE LITTLE "DIFFERENCES" BETWEEN SCIENCE AND FOLKLORE 27
  AND SO THEY CELEBRATE PAGAN DAYS IN OUR PUBLIC SCHOOLS 31
  WHO GETS HURT IF OUR WITCHCRAFT IS TAKEN FROM US? 35
  A WITCH CASE IN THE MAKING--THAT NEVER WENT TO COURT (YET)! 38

WHAT MAKES A MAN SUPERSTITIOUS; HIS RELIGION, OR A LACK OF IT?

"THERE'S WITCHCRAFT IN PENNSYLVANIA AND WHEREVER ELSE YOU WANT TO FIND IT--IN AMERICA!" "Preposterous;" "I don't believe it;" "Impossible;" "Nothing to it;" "Well, I know where;" "They say it's true;" "She's an old Witch," or, "He's a Devil"-- sayings like these may be heard on all sides when a subject such as this is brought up.

"There may have been 'witchcraft' of a sort a few generations ago, but is this still practiced among the Pennsylvania Germans?" is not an uncommon query when strangers come into the Keystone State.

Quite often, yes, more frequently than not, you will get an affirmative reply from those who profess to know something about such matters. Furthermore, there is considerable basis in fact for the general belief that "witchcraft" still prevails in one of the most enlightened states and sections of the country.

But why does it "hang on?"

Why?--Persistency in any form of witchcraft as it prevails in the minds of men and women today, is that they haven't taken steps to inquire into the subject--as to whether there is really any such thing as a "witch," and, what it might be.

Let us carefully examine what we can learn about them, as defined in the "Century Dictionary:"

Witch, n. A man or woman. 1. A person (of either sex) given to the black art; a sorcerer; a conjuror; a wizard; later and more particularly, a woman supposed to have formed a compact with the devil or with evil spirits, and to be able by their aid to operate supernaturally; one who practises sorcery or enchantment; a sorceress.

2. An old, ugly, and crabbed or malignant woman; a hag; a crone: a term of abuse.

3. A fascinating woman; a woman, especially a young woman or a girl, possessed of peculiar attractions, whether of beauty or of manners; a bewitching or charming young woman or girl.

4. A charm or spell.

The reader will note, and it may be generally recognized that not only an ugly woman, but a young, attractive one, too, can bewitch, or be bewitching; i. e., "do things to you!" This is a radical departure from the general belief that only old women, or sometimes old men, can "bewitch."

These refer to witches in the flesh; then there are those which cannot be seen, but according to some people, can be felt; i. e., can do bodily harm, though they are only of the "spirit."

The "Century Dictionary" says still further, regarding an

Apparition, n. An appearance, epiphany, also attendants. 1. The act of appearing or coming into sight; appearance; the state of being visible; visibility. 2. That which appears or becomes visible; an appearance, especially of a remarkable or phenomenal kind. Specifically--3. A ghostly appearance; a specter or phantom: now the usual sense of the word.

It will serve to keep the record straight to review briefly the meaning of Superstition, n. An ignorant or irrational fear of that which is unknown or mysterious; especially, such fear of some invisible existence or existences; specifically, religious belief or practice, or both, founded on irrational fear or credulity; excessive or unreasonable religious scruples produced by credulous fears.

"Where there is any religion, the devil will plant superstition," says Burton, in "Anatomy of Melancholy."

Lowell says, in "Among My Books," first series, (p. 92): "A superstition, as it's name imports, is something that has been left over, like unfinished business, from one session of the world's witenagemot to the next."

One cannot be sure at all as to how many sessions of the world's "witenagemot" we have already had, but, whatever the number, we still have the fears of men and women, scarcely alleviated in all the history of the world. After life, death--then what? We have assurances of all kinds, to be sure, but, as individuals we have yet to test these assurances!

The philosophy of many centuries that instilled both hope and fear into the heart of man, left him with the two well known spirits to swing and sway his thoughts, as we see the swaying of leaves on the trees.

Frankly, can there be any religion or philosophy which does not preach or teach that there is good and bad, both?--that if we have "angels" we must have "witches" or some other equivalent to offset the other force?

We have in Pennsylvania, and in America, many men and women who belong to the same church as their parents and grandparents, which brings out the thought we have in mind, viz: "What was good enough for them is good enough for me!"

Mosaic Influence Still Impelling.--Our social and religious backgrounds are primarily Mosaic--where-ever we find ourselves in the Western civilization. Yet Moses, whoever he was, had to rescue what he could in philosophy and truth from a past fraught with pagan ideas. Many of those old pagan ideas are today still our ideas.

It requires little knowledge to satisfy the average person that it is very difficult, if not impossible to put one's fingers on a "spirit" (or a "soul")--yet, isn't that what we do when we "dissect" such ideas as witches, angels, and souls, and tell our friends that we have been, or others have been "visited" by angels, or witches--or that a "certain soul" actually went to heaven, or to hell?

It is a certainty that men and women over-imagine too many ideas dealing with things and ideas, not actually of the solid earth; or that cannot be taken apart and analyzed.

As defined by the dictionary, we, too, are in hearty accord in the conclusion that witchcraft is derived from "suppositions," "suggestions," "imaginations," or "pipe-dreams" of simple folk.

Now "simple folk" are not always to be indicated as being persons who do not agree with the personal views of the reader, or the writer!

There are many professional men and women whose manners and conduct in life suggest to the layman that there can be "simpleness" among the learned, too!

WITCHCRAFT AND BELIEFS IN EVIL SPIRITS CAME TO AMERICA LONG AGO

WITCHES Active in Middle Ages.--In the middle ages in Europe there was great activity in "witchcraft." Then came a time when the Popes took cognizance of the practices to which the layman of the church, and outsiders, were resorting--certain functions generally reserved for the priesthood.

Following Papal Bulls in 1233 and 1484, thousands upon thousands of innocent people were put to death, as they are in Europe today--because they happened to live at the time some "master" of misguided religious or political philosophy cared little whether the people "would be better off dead, than alive."

There may be considerable division among people relative to the term "witch;" some will want to class it with devils, or demons. There may be other forms which some would want to employ to describe the opposite of an angel. Now, so far as most of us are concerned, the latter have been described largely through artists' conceptions, which, as in the case of devils, leave much in doubt, and to the imagination as well.

Europeans Knew About Witches.--The earliest settlers of America--Spanish, English, Dutch, Swedes, French, German, etc., all had a "working knowledge," generally speaking, of religious backgrounds, especially respecting good and bad--angels and witches. Most of the books brought to America by either of the above races were of a religious nature, having, of course, general rules for religious behavior, if not of a moral and civil behavior, as well.

Today, as in the earliest colonial days, it matters little whether one gets his religious knowledge in the public schools, or parochial schools; in the home, or directly from religious publications.

The knowledge available to all, even to the unlearned, or unschooled, is so widespread as to convey certain religious philosophies to the layman.

He doesn't have to know the law of God, nor of man, to understand that the normal laws of society forbid that he should kill his fellow man. Some are thus held in restraint, but when a man wants to kill--he'll do it!

But one of the sins of society is that so many men (and women) of sound mental knowledge and able to reason, are killers, and who escape the just punishment for their crime. "Extenuating circumstances;" "passion;" "mentally unsound;" and "drunkenness!" We would like to use a remark attributed to the late President Lincoln, which propriety forbids our using here; it isn't often that his language may be too expressive--even if only about "horses."

Bible Basis for Strong Beliefs.--If a christian anywhere, particularly a protestant christian, wishes to know the fundamental law on "behavior" he sooner or later goes to the Scriptures for "light." Surely the reader will not question our ethics in bringing this phase of the subject to any one's attention.

Rev. P. Marion Simms, Ph. D., in his very enlightening and comprehensive account of "The Bible in America," says:

The Roman Catholic Church and the Protestant Church differ in many things, but nowhere more widely than the place they assign the Bible, and in the right of its private interpretation . . . By this means they (the former) think to avoid the dangers involved . . .

The old time conception, once held well-nigh universally among Christians, that the Bible is the very Word of God, verbally dictated by the Lord hiniself and infallible in its every statement, has been responsible for more misuse of the Bible than all other influences put together . . .

Therefore, with entire consistency, "Thou shalt not suffer a witch to live," (Exodus 22:18) was made the basis of the persecution of witches, with all its horrors. This Scripture was the chief authority for the execution of witches everywhere; and it is only a modified conception of the Bible that can release the church from the obligation of witch hunting today. Changing the translation to "sorceress" does not affect the authority of the commandment . . . The stories of the persecution of witches and that of the Inquisition could be written only with a pen dipped in blood and tears and yet it came legitimately from the old time conception and interpretation of the Bible. All persecutions by Christians in America, as elsewhere, were supported always by quotations from the Bible.

And so, because it is true that the vast majority of the early settlers of America were men who read the Bible, and imparted its truths and lessons of all kinds to their children, and no less to their grandchildren, we have today in America, the hodge-podge which was Europe. The various races have handed to each succeeding generation their pet notions in everything.

Do we know any Irish who are not "in love" with old Irish traditions; Slav with Slavish; Norse with Norse; Latin with Latin? You can answer this from your own observations. The Anglo-Saxon is proud of notions and ideals he can recall; so is the Jew; and so is the Negro. Traditions are hard to change, or forget.

Today we are reaping, as each generation does, that portion of knowledge which was sown early in the dawn of history, and as it ripens and falls into the minds of young and old everywhere, we shall accordingly stand or fall by our decisions to be rational, or irrational--"orthodox," or "unorthodox."

PURITANS RAISED HELL WITH WITCHES IN EARLY DAYS

SALEM Witches Were Hanged.--The witches of our own New England were largely the development of too-serious interpretations of Biblical law and injunction; actually, by law, authorities (under pressure of the church leaders) took numerous lives of innocent people.

Religion Cause of the Troubles.--One can hardly picture witchcraft conditions in those early days as being so serious that nearly every man, woman and child, and everything in the catalog of human knowledge was suspected of being a witch, or in aiding one.

To avoid being accused as a witch, one had to get "the jump on the other fellow" and accuse him first!

Montague Summers, in "The Geography of Witchcraft," at p. 256 says: "There can be no doubt that the settlers in New England were not only firm believers in every kind of witchcraft, but well primed in every malevolent superstition that could commend itself to their prejudiced and tortured minds. They looked for the Devil round every corner, and saw Satan's hand in every mishap, in every accident. The Devil, in fact, played a larger part in their theology than God. They were obsessed with hell and damnation; their sky was cloudy and overset; their horizon girded with predestination and the awful consciousness of sin."

John Wesley was a firm believer in witchcraft, and in 1768 he writes in his journal: "It is true . . . that the English in general . . . have given up all accounts of witches and apparitions as mere old wives' fables. I am sorry for it . . . With my latest breath will I bear testimony against giving up to infidels one great proof of the invisible world: I mean that of witchcraft and apparitions, confirmed by the testimony of all ages."

In New England one person claimed that the Devil frequently had carnal knowledge of her body!

Today houses are still secured, as well as barns, day and night, against witches. Window blinds, or shutters keep out all light, and some occupants have been known to go out very seldom, after dark--the darkness that harbors all sorts of things, only through imagination.

Today some people can hear witches in chains, or shutters rattling at night; chairs or floors creaking; noises in the walls, attics or cellars; lowing of cattle; howling of dogs; earth lights in the fields or woods, or in the cemetery; shadows in the moonlight; strange odors; the noise of expansion or contraction of pottery, or steam pipes; the noise caused by mice, rats, and slight vibrations caused by draughts.

Likewise, Pennsylvania has been singled out for years as a stamping ground for these same kind of "devils." Research, however, fails to discover any witches, looking any different from the people the reader and the writer know most intimately; now and then an old man, or woman, may be identified as "one of those 'witch doctors,' or 'pow-wow' doctors." But, in New England, well-known citizens were pointed out as "witches."

Sydney George Fisher, in "Men, Women and Manners in Colonial Times," (2 vols. Phila. 1898) says:

"In former times no sect of religion and no class of life had been free from it (witchcraft), more than four thousand books had been written about it, it had assailed the highest intellectuals as well as the lowest, and Sprenger estimates that in the fifteenth century one hundred thousand persons were executed for it in Germany alone, and that during the Christian epoch nine million men and women had been put to death for this supposed crime. Those who doubted were reminded of the witch of Endor in the Old Testament and of the laws of Moses against witchcraft. In the books of the Middle Ages it is asserted over and over again that to doubt the existence of witchcraft is to deny the Holy Scriptures and to refuse confidence in the general belief of all mankind."

". . . No one was safe; the slightest peculiarity in manner, or an obscure chance remark that could be given a double meaning, was enough to secure a conviction. Many who had lost some household article or cattle, or who had suffered a misfortune or sickness, were allowed to relate their trouble before the court as evidence that one of their neighbors had bewitched them . . . When a person was accused, his only hope of escape was in confession, and this process manufactured witches very fast. . ."

"Even in this awful delusion the Puritan mind still worked by its close reasoning processes. The few who were opposed to punishing for witchcraft argued that it might be possible for a devil to get into a person and make a witch of him against his will . . . "

"If an ordinary man, they said, does anything supernatural, it must be by aid of the devil . . ."

In Pennsylvania the authorities always gave, and today give, the accused the great benefit of doubt--either as to the commission of a crime (of witchcraft), or the mental state of the person involved. Is witchcraft in this Commonwealth, then, so very terrible?

Mary Baker Eddy--and Witchcraft.--Howard W. Haggard, M. D., in "Devils, Drugs and Doctors," (at pp. 312-3; Blue Ribbon Books, Inc.) tells how Mary Baker Eddy, in her own day, put a lot of faith in the powers of "malicious animal magnetism"--just another term for witchcraft. Mrs. Eddy, according to a newspaper account, declared that her husband's death was caused by this "magnetism"--the opposite of faith healing. Dr. Haggard further states:

Thus when Mary Eddy assigned hysterical ailments to malicious animal magnetism and asked the courts of Salem, in 1878, to punish alleged persecutors, she was attempting to revive witchcraft and the punishment of witches. But along with this black magic she introduced white magic . . .

STRANGE EVOLUTION FOR GETTING RID OF EVIL SPIRITS

CHASING Witches a Religious Rite.--Witches can make themselves "at home" in many ways. According to a "ritual" of Jewish behavior, it appears witches can get into clothes and into man over night; lying-in women should be apprehensive of "evil spirits," hence magic words are prepared for such as lie-in. Christians use Bibles under their pillows, and Catholics use medals, beads, or prayer-books for a similar purpose.

Orthodox Jews believe that witches abound in heaps of rubbish, or in bunches of tops of vegetables, if thrown away together; egg shells must be broken; witches can harm a person, alone, in darkness, but not if there are two or three persons together; a burning light is proof against evil spirits.

Have we not heard of many of these same "notions" among people not of Jewish extraction?

What makes a man or woman superstitious? His religion, or lack of it?

Several particularly impressive evidences of a belief in witches, or witchcraft, may be cited.

The custom of the Orthodox Jews, Catholics and Protestant layman are compared, as excerpted from a book on the Jews:

The next Holy-day is call'd "Sookoth," i. e. Tabernacle or Booth, see Leviticus, Chap. xxiii. 34. This Holy-day they celebrate eight Days, tho' but seven are commanded in Levit. xxiii. because of the Uncertainty from which of the two Days of their New Year they are to begin their Reckoning; during which eight Days they eat and drink, and some even sleep, every Night in their Tabernacles, see Levit. xxiii. 42, and in their Synagogues they have a Citron in their left Hand, and a Branch of a Palm-tree in their right Hand; to which Branch they tye a Bunch of thick Boughs of Myrtle, see Levit. xxiii, 40, and with these Weapons in Hand, they hold both their Hands close together, and whilst the Reader sings the "Howdoo" in the "Hollel," and the "Hoseana," they exercise with the Palm-branch, shaking the Point of it first three times towards the East, then three times towards the South, then three times towards the West, then three times towards the North; then three times towards the Heavens, and last of all, three times towards the Earth; whereby they suppose to chace away all the evil Spirits hovering about the Synagogue to intercept their Prayers, and hinder them from going up to Heaven.

(Chasing evil spirits away has been the business of man since "witches" were invented in the Old Testament. In addition to the Jews, Catholic clergymen "shake" a ritualistic object to "bless" the individual, the automobile, the firemen and police force, or whatever is to be "blessed." The motion of the "magic wand" and use of magical words in Latin create a ring of angels about the object of blessing--a ring so great and strong that "evil spirits" cannot get close (so long as the angels are not caught unawares--which blessings last no longer than one year.) The result is that blessings, like oil, will float constantly "on top," while they last. We have seen exactly the same method of procedure caught by a news-reel movie man in a back-woods settlement in north central Pennsylvania a few years ago, when a man of little or no religious conviction "chased the witches" away from his home (with a wave of his hands and in unintelligible words just like the priest's)--without the benefit of clergy! From whence came his ideas, his methods, and his "power?" The menace which he sought to dissolve, has not returned to his ramshackle mountain hut; for if it had we would have seen it in the papers!--Editor. From "Little Known Facts About the Ritual of the Jews and the Esoteric Folklore of the Pennsylvania-Germans;" published by The Aurand Press, Harrisburg, Pa., 1939).

From these brief evidences of Jewish and Catholic service, whether to bless or chase away, we have every reason to suppose that the backwoodsman (who probably was a "poor Protestant"), had hope in his mind when be deliberately charged in four directions with a distinct "E-yah; E-yah," for each motion, and, to most readers of this account, his "ritual" would have had as much meaning as if they had attended services in a Catholic church or a synagogue.

Are we to suppose, and conclude, that the layman's "prayers" would go unanswered, while the ordained and official servants could actually obtain intercessions? What do you conclude? If this backwoodsman's prayers are of no likely success, what impels you to think that you, or any other person speaking for you, can gain a favorable ear, where prayers are "heard?"

Beliefs of Early Penna. Germans.--Julius Friedrich Sachse, in "The German Pietists of Provincial Pennsylvania," gives an interesting word picture of the early days. In part he says:

Another custom then in vogue among the Germans in Pennsylvania was the wearing of an "anhangsel," a kind of astrological amulet or talisman . . . In rare cases a thin stone or sheet of metal was used in place of parchment. These "anhangsel," or "zauber-zettel" as they were called, were prepared by the Mystics of the Community with certain occult ceremonies at such times as the culmination of a particular star or the conjunction of certain planets . . . (and) supposed to exercise an extraordinary influence over the destiny of the bearer, particularly in averting disease, checking the power of evil spirits, and defending the wearer from malice and all harm . . . hardly an adult or child was to be found without one . . . Frequently a charm of this kind would be placed upon an infant immediately upon its birth, as well as upon a corpse prior to interment . . .

Independent of the above described charms and talismans, there was another kind of superstition common to the general populace. This was known as "besprechen," a kind of conjuration for the cure of wounds or minor diseases in both man and beast. The ceremony was nearly always performed by an old man or woman, usually the latter . . . (and) that to maintain their efficiency they (the formulae) had to be handed down by an alternation of the sexes.

We may easily assume that the old man or woman who might thus be called on to "extend sympathy," were venerable, in a sense, and a fair substitute for the occasional itinerant minister, or preacher, or the physician still more difficult to have, when distance and impracticability had to be reckoned with. If these old "venerables" were satisfactory "in a pinch," as we say, would they be less so at any other time of need?

CHARMS AND TRINKETS ARE REVERED BY MANY OF OUR PEOPLE

MANY Charms May be Used.--We mention but a few good luck and health charms, all worn in the hope of avoiding evil, or ill-health--which is just another name for evil (witches).

There is the garlic sack; onions; stockings; the bag or sack with hot bacon and pepper; the crucifix; medals which have been blessed; a parchment containing prayers, etc.; bones, teeth and many other items--all more or less "witch" charms.

It may not be amiss to remind the reader that one can scarcely ever find a Catholic of Irish or Italian or other extraction, who is not wearing a charm suspended from his neck, one near the heart, or carrying one in pocket or purse. Likewise, it is easy to find many charms, blessed by a priest for a dollar or two, affixed to automobiles owned or driven by Catholic drivers.

It is fair play for us to declare that if they feel that some good will come from wearing these charms, then by the same sign they will not need to fear any evil. It is the old story all over again--one man's meat may be another man's poison! The reader and a lot of his relatives do lots of things the Jew and the Catholic do not find in harmony with their philosophy.

Old World, and New World Charm.--"Letters of Protection" as we know them in America, or sometimes "Himmelsbriefs" as they are known both here and in Germany, are quite common in America, or were not many years ago.

Many Pennsylvania German homes have a large, or perhaps a smaller copy, framed as others would have, for instance, the "Lord's Prayer," or the motto "God Bless Our Home"--all having the same end in view. But an English version of the "Himmelsbrief" also received a large circulation, as late as 1918, during the world war of that time and since then.

We accepted an order for printing copies of the "Letter of Protection" in 1918, which we learned were subsequently handed to members of the National Guard, and to draftees who went into the service from several central counties of Pennsylvania.

These charms were limited in their circulation to friends of the party for whom we did the printing.

Since that date, however, we have learned a great deal more about "witchcraft" as an age-old subject, and its comforting assurance to those who are protected while carrying such charm--no less than the Catholic who has his charm constantly on him, or her.

Quoting from C. J. S. Thompson's book, "Mysteries and Secrets of Magic," at page 270, we read of one of these letters written by a Pope for a Kingly subject, as follows:

According to the writer of this manuscript, King Charles I is said to have carried a charm against danger and poison that was written for him by Pope Leo IX. It was inscribed as follows:

"Who that beareth it upon him shall not dread his enemies, to be overcome, nor with no manner of poison be hurt, nor in no need misfortune, nor with no thunder he shall not be smitten nor lightning, or in no fire be burnt soddainly, nor in no water be drowned. Nor he shall not die without shrift, nor with theeves to be taken. Also he shall have no wrong neuther of Lord or Lady. This be in the names of God and Christ ✠ Messias ✠ Sother ✠ Emannell ✠ Saibaoth ✠ "

Locks Keep Out the Witches.--In "Olden Times; or, Pennsylvania Rural Life, Some Fifty Years Ago," by H. L. Fisher, Esq., (York, Pa., 1888), appear a great many poems. Part of one of them reveals the attitude of most rural folk a century ago, when it was quite the proper thing for preachers to excite their people with stories about "fire and brimstone," and perhaps "hell and damnation;" "angels and devils, or satan (witches)." Where does one go nowadays to hear sermons of this sort. Says Mr. Fisher, in part:

> Whether scripture was read, or prayers were said,
> Is more than the writer remembers;
> But it runs in his head, ere the two went to bed,
> They carefully covered the embers.
>
> Yea, even much more--they locked every door
> Upon horses, cows, heifers and stirks;
> The house-doors were barred and the gateways tarred,
> Thus, showing their faith in their works.
>
> What more could be done? Smith loaded his gun
> With powder and ball and with shot;
> "Near the head of my bed I'll have it," he said,
> "And for witches and thieves make it hot."
>
> Gun loaded and cocked and all the doors locked,
> Let witches and thieves do their best,
> Gates bolted and barred, and some even tarred,
> Man and beast might slumber and rest.

SOME OF THE "FAMOUS" WITCH TRIALS IN PENNSYLVANIA

EARLY Witch Trial in Pennsylvania.--To illustrate the extremely fortunate circumstances in having so few witch trials in Pennsylvania, we bring to you reference to the first reported case (which turned out to be not much of a case at all), in which William Penn sat in judgment--and let it speak for itself.

There is in our "'Pow Wow' Book," (The Aurand Press, Harrisburg, 1929), a detailed account of what appears to be the only "witch" trial in the entire history of the Colony, Province or the Commonwealth of Pennsylvania.

Margaret Mattson and Yeshro Hendrickson, (Swedish women), had been accused as witches, and the jury accordingly found a true bill. Absentee jurymen were fined 40 shillings each!

The first mentioned pleaded "not guilty" to the charge that she bewitched calves, geese, etc., but that, while she could bewitch cattle, oxen were above her reach. Her daughter's suspicions and convictions were given in evidence, but "the prisoner denieth all things."

Governor Penn charged the jury, which brought in a verdict sufficiently ambiguous and ineffective for such a dubious offense, saying they find her "guilty of having the common fame of a witch, but not guilty in the manner and form as she stands indicted." The women were put on their good behavior for six months!

It may be pointed out that in the early days of the colony, we had by precedent, a statute of King James I. "That act," says Watson in his "Annals of Philadelphia and Pennsylvania," "was held to be part of our law by an act of our provincial Assembly, entitled 'An Act against conjuration, witchcraft and dealing with evil and wicked spirits.'"

But all around us in the early days one heard of witches and witchcraft--Virginia, New Jersey, New York, and New England. Where, even today, is there a State, or Nation, wherein one cannot find such beliefs? Folklore and customs are long-lasting; because we have never learned of such things is a poor assumption that there is no "such thing."

The Penn decision reminds one of the account of Jesus in the Temple, writing on the ground with his finger, and saying, as we read in John 8:7: ". . . He that is without sin among you, let him first cast a stone at her . . . 9. And they which heard it, being convicted by their own conscience, went out one by one. . ."

Several "Near" Witch Trials.--The case of the York boys, three of them, who murdered an old man for a book, or a lock of hair, back in 1928, is well known throughout America. It was about that time that newspapers needed some innoculations in the matter of a new line of news, and the York case certainly went a long way to fill the bill.

Subsequently a baby at Lebanon died of malnutrition, and again the "witch doctor" got it in the neck, and the newspapers got the "news."

In the same neighborhood a "buried treasure" hoax got abroad, and "headlines" got a lot of "hex" ideas across.

A case in Lehigh county tried to rear its head a dozen years ago, but if it was a "witch" case they are still trying to solve it.

Then there was the Bechtel case in Philadelphia--a Mennonite who was murdered--the authorities at first declaring it was witchcraft--which it wasn't.

Murder "For Insurance" Is Hardly "Witchcraft."--Recently closing its records, the Philadelphia courts charged a number of persons with "witchcraft," or, at least that was the impression left after reading the newspapers. The cases turned out to be nothing more than mere "murder-for-insurance"--surely a long way off from "witchcraft."

The Shinsky Case in 1934.--There was the case of Albert Shinsky, near Pottsville--notable for the fact that he claimed he killed a witch in self-defense--and, that nothing whatsoever happened in that affair to prove, or disprove, the theory regarding witches, other than that they are creatures of the mind, and of that fact there is little, or no doubt.

Newspapers at that time published a copyright account by this writer, some of them with screaming headlines: "Did Bible Figure in Witch Slaying?"

In the article thus published, we had not established positively that the Bible did figure, but suggested "it could have;" this conclusion was supported a few days later when a professor from a Philadelphia university, accompanied by an officer, called on Shinsky in his jail cell.

Warden William Watson, of the Schuylkill county prison, reported that Albert Shinsky believed that the murder of Mrs. Mummey, a "witch," was justified in the Bible. Warden Watson was quoted in the Phila. "Inquirer," of March 26, 1934, as follows:

"He told me," said the Warden, "that there are numerous instances in the Scriptures where the sacrifice of human life has been declared necessary. He cited the Old Testament tale of how Abraham was about to kill his son Isaac on the altar as showing the necessity for taking human life to placate spiritual curses or spells.

"He told me that all the New Testament writers clearly believed in the power of demons and that the devil is a real personage, and not merely an evil influence as modern theologists have it.

"The Bible represents the devil as a fallen angel, who goes about whispering and suggesting evil acts. If you will read closely you will find that Hell was made for the torment of the devil, and not human beings, as a way of escape from that place has been provided for all of us."

An eminent psychiatrist, Dr. A. I. Baron, of Philadelphia, who examined Shinsky in jail, reports that

"When I left his cell after an exhaustive research as far back as his earliest memories, I knew that I had been talking to an adolescent boy of the most primitive development. I had been talking with a mental and emotional infant.

"If the State demands the death penalty for Schuylkill county's 'hex' slayer, society will be seeking revenge upon a 13-year-old savage."

Dr. Barton reported that Shinsky, although 23 years old, "has actually been five different people, each personally at war with the other four;" that he was "in medical phraseology--an emotional, imaginative extrovert with schizophrenic reactions."

If psychiatrists were called in to examine 100, or 1000 adults, taken from the streets at random, we wonder how many of that number would have large traces of the same "disease" attributed to Shinsky. Surely the "things" he bred in his mind can be found in the minds of all too many others.

It is probably true, as pointed out elsewhere in this account, that "religion and superstition walk hand in hand;" that children learn about "this and that," but cannot, when they reach adulthood, separate their thoughts from those learned as a child. The general effects of this inability to forget surely has taken a terrible toll in the history of man.

Yet, on the other hand, if we could forget as easily as would be necessary to get rid of witches, we would as likely forget to whom we are married, whose kids belong to who, and certainly where we live!

Whether Mrs. Mummey was a witch, or not, we'll never know-- and the authorities sent Albert to a place for men with "weak minds."

The Late Clarence Darrow, Esq., Was Interested in the York "Witch" Case

The late Clarence G. Darrow, eminent lawyer and scholar, is quoted in reference to the York witchcraft case, at the sentencing of 14-year-old John Curry, to "life in prison."

"Outrage," is the one word expressed by Darrow, who then queried: "Do you think the State of Pennsylvania will stand for it? . . . It seems a terrible outrage." Yes, the State did stand for it, although, after something like ten years Curry was released from the penitentiary.

While many persons did not like all of Darrow's opinions, nevertheless he was a deep thinker, and we record here his opinions regarding the York case, as reported in the Harrisburg "Patriot," Feb. 21, 1929:

"Belief in witchcraft cannot, in itself, be thought a crime. If it is there would be but few of us really innocent. Not so many years ago our best people and devout Christians not only believed in witches but guaranteed their celestial happiness by murdering them.

"We placidly admit that there are sections of our country where people are isolated by their own customs and thought, or by geography, and live quaintly a century and a half behind our little more enlightened communities. But we forget that a mere century and a half takes us almost back to Cotton Mather and the stake. Then witches were hanged for the glory of God and for the peace of mind of those who thought they had been or might be bewitched. There are today groups of people who have advanced but little in mentality beyond the ignorant frenzy that glorified in hangings.

"Even today a literal interpretation of the Bible would force us to believe in witchcraft and sorcery. And those simple folk of which that Curry boy is a product hold strictly to the Word just as they find it. To them the Witch of Endor is very real. The devil is real. Spells are real. In their world, furnished by traditions, myths and Old World lore, handed down unchanged from one generation to another, there are evil spirits as certain as a flying railroad train bearing down on a motorist stalled on the tracks.

"Is there any doubt that Curry and those others believed that Rehmeyer had an evil power which he could exercise at will? Is there any doubt that they thought a lock of his hair would break the spell? Nothing new in that belief, nothing unusual. Reach into your own pocket for your own personal protector against bad luck.

"Our belief in capital punishment as a deterrent is just another form of witchcraft. Apart from the mass desire for revenge, there is a subconscious desire to rid ourselves of what we believe to be an evil person. We look in vain for any proof that executions have had any effect on crime. When England punished by death everything from bread and sheep stealing to wholesale killing, crime was far more general than it is today. Education and the training of youth in trades and profession has diminished crime, never the death penalty.

"Isn't there every reason to believe that the crime of murder is a symptom. In the York case it was clearly a symptom of a prevailing ignorance, a condition which should never be allowed to exist in the State of Pennsylvania. . . ."

THOSE LITTLE "DIFFERENCES" BETWEEN SCIENCE AND FOLKLORE

NO Witches--No Angels.--The reader must reach this conclusion in his own reasoning--we are not intent on persuading you to believe something you do not want to believe; persuasions are not made that way. If we do not have witches, as some would tell us, then we cannot have angels, according to those others who feel they do some thinking, too. Denying the one, and not excluding the other, makes a man's everyday reasoning look silly, does it not?

When we compare notes with men of the cloth, as to the possibility of there being witches in the world, and here at home, they usually greet the comment with a rather blank expression, but no rebuttal.

Yet, it just must be true that we do have witches and "witchcraft" in Pennsylvania--in and out of religious circles--for we have great faith and belief in the presence and power of angels--not only those that hovered over the hills of Judea, but also the red and blue hills of our beloved Pennsylvania!

To accept belief in one element and not in the other would tend to destroy the joys of many holidays fostered by the Christian church.

State to Banish Belief in Witches.--One of the most interesting news items we have seen in two score years, appeared in one of the Harrisburg papers a few years ago. It was inspired in one of the highest state departments, but got out of the department, into the papers, without the head-man knowing anything about it (so he said). This is the item; read it thoroughly:

SEE EDUCATION ENDING 'HEX' BELIEFS IN PENNA.

Harrisburg (during the Earle Administration).--State educators declared here yesterday that hexerei, terror of numerous rural farm communities for many years, is being banished from Pennsylvania by the public schools.

School authorities explained that instruction in the sciences, even in the lower grades, has proved the most effective weapon against the superstition.

They said that "hex" symbols calculated to cause illness in a farrn-house or disease of cattle still may be seen on farms and houses, but that the younger rural folk spurn beliefs that frightened their kin only a few years back.

Court records show the "hex" responsible for many crimes, including murder and arson, during the past 50 years.

Many items of news get into the papers--all types of stories--but it is noteworthy to record that some one had in mind becoming a new Savior of the human race!

How in the world are the school authorities going to do all this? Do they think that children will remember only what they learn in school, and forget all they learn at home, in the Sunday-school, church, in the theatres, AND on the streets?

Will the schools teach a new truth--that "all is good"--"nothing is evil?"--and won't the kids forget? With teachers who are recruited from every type of religion, some anti-religious, and some too religious, what impress will that make on the student, as against "science?"

Will the public school system evolve a new plan of study that will prove the stories in the Bible to be something different than children have been led to believe--for years?

And, what will the new studies have to say on the subject of, let us say: "holy-water," as used by the Catholics in their devotions; or, even plain water, as used by the Protestants in their baptism ceremonies?

If the schools must support this phase of religion and its symbolism, will they declare that water for baptisms, or holy-water, are efficacious when used in a religious sense, and not be of effect when used by "witch doctors" either at home, or abroad?

Science already agrees that there is no value to either of these waters, or services, but if it is forced down the throats of youngsters in school, it will upset the plans of the church fathers of all creeds! The latter claim that holy-water, accompanied by "prayers," has a special virtue that beats anything science has yet produced! Can school-learning overcome this belief?

The science which the school authorities are teaching is a poor science that says "hex" slayings and practices, are so much more vicious and devastating in Pennsylvania, than "sex" slayings and their many practices; so much more degrading and superstitious than the thousand and one promises delivered from a hundred thousand platforms in America and throughout the world, which never come true; and worse than the countless self-abuses of which they say little or nothing--and certainly not in the public press.

The State and school authorities flounder in their own mire when they fail to recognize that many of our superstitions are condoned and taught within church and school, and which, per se, makes them "perfect" (or "white art"); but when practised outside church or school, makes them "black art."

Let us talk about "hallowe'en," the season when witches, vampire bats, black cats, and fantastics with their false-faces and hideous make-up, are abroad in all America. Where, if you please, do we see greater evidences of a survival of the idea of "witches" than in the grade schools of America?

We received a number of very interesting comments from well known Americans on the subject of "Science vs. Witches--in the Schools." Some are from physicians, professors, educators, writers, and just plain everyday citizens.

AND SO THEY CELEBRATE PAGAN DAYS IN OUR PUBLIC SCHOOLS

OCTOBER 31 a Fertile Day for Witches.--On Hallowe'en teachers and parents encourage, and children indulge their whole hearts and minds in celebrating this event. Doubtless very few teachers, certainly not very many parents, and hardly any youngsters know anything about the feast they thus celebrate. If it was originally a pagan rite, are we but little different--or can we throw it off next year, and forget it forever?

All of them go to no end of trouble to cut out black cats, witches, and by their fantastic dress, mock a day that the educators have told us they will "banish from the schools!" Well, why don't they?

Some tell us that the way it is celebrated today is just a "mockery" of the past! What is the point in it? Many of the silly things of today are "mockeries of the past." In the midst of all this tom-foolery there are some children who get "notions" about witches and superstitions that they will never forget to their dying day.

If they were never to hear of these things, they, when they arrive at manhood and womanhood, especially parenthood, would never need, nor could they transmit these foolish ideas to their off-spring. We have all too many games and friendly arguments, started "all in fun," ending in disaster. We have seen little tots scared almost stiff at fantastic false-faces; what good can come from these festivals?

Thoughts of witches and the like, whether referred to in the Bible, or in ordinary conversation, are not always taken too lightly, even on festive occasions.

Whistling in the dark, for instance, is one form of driving away fear; denial of witches by some may be an outward and spoken manifestation of non-belief, but our people do not always tell, or act, the truth, and the reader knows this only too well.

One may observe this on Easter and Christmas, when we deliberately make up characters--legendary--for those occasions--so that we all know that much which is told to children is not true--and it is safe to say that many things the children tell their folks--are short of the truth! If little white lies are justifiable on those occasions, are they not suitable on other occasions. And what about the black ones?

Fears Come Easy to Children.--Fear, as of thunder and lightning, may be acquired in the natural course of life, but youngsters too often get such fears from solicitous, or nervous, and superstitious parents, generally the mother, who is the nearest thing on earth to being a Diety that any child can have.

Fear, as of things in the dark, when one is alone, is as old as Jewish, or even pagan history. Where two or more are together in the dark, witches cannot do any harm! In this idea we see the birth of "misery loves company."

The demand of youngsters that some one "turn on the light," or "light a lamp, or candle," before they enter a dark room, is just as much a terror to those of today as it was in the author's day. Some of us demanded that a light be allowed to burn all night. What could we be afraid of, except "evil spirits" in the dark? We weren't afraid of "angels!" A fear of "something in the dark," is almost universal!

Modern Hallowe'en Witches.--Now witches, in the flesh, or in the spirit, are always out to do harm, or so it would appear. Take youngsters, or grown-ups around the time of Hallowe'en; they can write on walls, windows, automobiles, and sidewalks, and the words they spell out are rarely used by nice people (in public).

Much property is damaged, some carted away to be found weeks later; men and women get drunk, and celebrate orgies not unlike the eve of Mayday in England and Scotland, a century ago, or festivals in ancient Rome.

None of the devilment of this season is at all necessary, so one has the right to feel that "witches" do live and cause all kinds of trouble; they rarely are caught. They may be only embryos now, but give them time, they'll grow--and their off-spring annoy others! And the school system helps, aids and abets!

Physicians Uphold "Pow Wow" Doctors.--Science may claim to stand on its own feet, and may agree with the history of past ages in certain cases, but there must be a parting of the ways sooner or later, if science attempts to destroy some of the fondest pets of the Christian civilization.

Even the medical profession took a hand in the matter recently when some of their learned authorities upheld the psychology that certain practices of the humble "pow wow" doctor have virtues that cannot be attained by either physician or priest!

Educators perhaps fail to appreciate the wisdom of Horace, who says: "Mingle a little folly with thy wisdom." They think (or do they?) that a child can play with fire, and, if burned, learn to stay away from fires. But "witches" and their kind are different kinds of fire. These children ought to grow up to be men and women--but how many of them do? How many of our adult population pass through life with 'teenage minds? If you want statistics on this, read the reports resulting from conscriptions for military service.

It is not our purpose to suggest to school authorities that they cease their attempts to discredit witches and the like; rather, it shows them what we think they have confronting them. But between "hex" and "sex" problems, we believe that the latter is the big job, and one they will have trouble to solve, if you gather what we mean.

When I was a child . . . I spake, understood, and thought as a child . . . but when I became a man . . . when I became a man . . . I put away childish things (I Cor. 13:11). When do boys become men . . . when do they forget the things they learned in their formative years? Do they forget . . . and cast them aside? . . . they do not! They pass them along to their sons and daughters . . . and they, in turn, to their sons and daughters . . . the superstitions and hexerei . . . and parts of the Ten Commandments . . . and the golden rule . . . whatever it may be . . . as they have for thousands of years . . . and when they grow up they will use modern science for what it will bring them in dollars and cents . . . but not as a rule to their faith and guide to their actions . . .

Who can look back over the years and say . . . "on that date I became a man!" . . . or, "then I became a woman!"

WHO GETS HURT IF OUR WITCHCRAFT IS TAKEN FROM US?

STUDENTS Afraid of This Subject.--Our interest in preparing this account is merely to "clear the atmosphere." A discourse dealing with the subject of witchcraft in Pennsylvania has been wanting for years.

We find ourselves in a pathetic sort of state, being associated with mature men and women who are actually afraid to delve into a subject as important as this is, because of a personal fear that something might "happen" to them! Conversation with many persons has borne out this conviction.

An interesting phase of this business of witchcraft, so far as it pertains to Pennsylvania, is just a lot of talk. In view of what has been said thus far, it might be good policy to illustrate what is meant when we say that witches and a belief in them will be hard to suppress.

First--There is no law against a belief in witches, or a practice of witchcraft--religious or civil;

Second--If there was a law, it would at once acknowledge that which many seek to deny really exists--witches--whether in the flesh, in spirit, or merely in mind.

Our Witches and Those of the Voodoo.--We should not confound the "witches" which our forefathers brought to America, with those under control of the witch-doctors and voodoos in the half-civilized areas as, in Africa, or the islands of the Caribbean, or South Seas; i. e., not too direct.

Our witches definitely have come to us through an association with emotions of good and bad, as we know them, through affiliates of the Christian church of all denominations-- Protestant, Catholic (Roman and Greek, or Eastern), and the Jews--or even the non-christian whose philosophies, in part, are like unto the Mosaic, in origin, viz: pagan. Perhaps, then, we have just bettered our very early ideas, and justified them for want of courage to change them! Is it reasonably safe to look at the customs, folklore, and superstitions of the African, and say to ourselves: "Well, that's about the way our folks looked at life not so very many generations ago!"

And yet, with all of this in mind, the witches of our time, and of the past, and those of the half-civilized native of Africa, Asia, and the islands, must have come from the same early pagan source--therefore we think it so strange that the Christian religion (of all religions) has given them any place at all--if there are no witches! All this despite the effort to destroy all books pertaining to the subject, as they tried to, at Ephesus.

The half-civilized, as well as the civilized, have a knowledge of, and emotions, which may be expressed by a reaction to favors received from good spirits, or bad spirits.

Do we have witches in Pennsylvania only among the Germanic people; not the English, Italian, Irish, Slav, Welsh, Hungarian, and the other races? How about the races in the forty-seven other states? Yes, how about them? And of more than two billion religious people in the world, not including the nonreligious? You say there are no witches today!!!

"Lord's Prayer" Says "Deliver Us From Evil."--Catholics and Protestants alike, in saying the Lord's Prayer, recognize something closely akin to everything in the catalog of the evil-spirit-world, no matter what name one may be pleased to call it--for do we not pray: "Deliver us from EVIL" . . .

This petition from the heart and mind of a Christian applies to the evils he or she concedes to be of any or every sort which might conceivably cause harm. Neither priest, preacher or scholar can explain this meaning "away" if the layman wants to believe it has a personal power for him!

A WITCH CASE IN THE MAKING--THAT NEVER WENT TO COURT (YET)!

MANY "Witch" Cases Never "Ripen."--While we have not recorded the complete history of witchcraft in Pennsylvania by any means, the reader will surely have attained some new slants on this vague subject. We cannot prove the existence, or non-existence, of either angels, or witches--neither can you!

Neither time, nor space, in a paper of this kind, will permit going into the highways and byways for all the rich, original accounts of past and present-day evidence of practices coming under this head. But we can offer just one or so, that have made their way to our "sanctum santorum."

Our Prize is from Dauphin County.--There is the Millersburg case. It is one of an old man who wanted to purchase a book, which he said would "break the spell on me." Claiming he already had several books which "could be used to break spells," none of them would work for him, and could we help him by providing the one he wanted? (Since we write, publish and sell books, it was a legitimate question). Perhaps we could, but first, "what seems to be the main trouble?" we inquired.

He told us he was "highly bewitched;" that "if she doesn't leave me alone I'll kill the son-of-a-----!"

We disliked seeing any person killed for no valid reason, yet set forth, worthy of death, so we inquired as to "Why do you want to kill some one--who is it?"

We could get no more out of him than the information that some woman, about middle age, was responsible for his "bewitchment."

We surmised he was a bachelor, and that he lived alone, which he subsequently confirmed; further, we deduced that the old fellow had not had much of nature's mating privileges. We had a "hunch" that he, being sex-starved, had "notions" concerning the woman, who was a widow; that, under the line of reasoning used by Benjamin Franklin, he was hopeful, she might, in her declining years prove more friendly, and eventually yield; failing to gain his point, his friendship turned to hate.

At long last we suggested we "might have" the right book, (which he seemed so anxious to own), if he would confide to us the nature of his complaint.

To the writer it seemed as if he was weighing our offer, and so in a few moments he bluntly replied: "Well, the old witch has me so fixed that I can't s----- (defecate) on Sundays and holidays!"

The reply was the "best" we had heard in a long while, but too good to laugh at, in his presence.

Assuming a rather "professional look," then a sort of secretive one, we said we could sympathize with him under such circumstances. He was serious, very serious, and we felt that he should be treated accordingly. Had we felt as he did (or had you), we would have wanted sympathy and--what he eventually got!

To sell him a book would have been the average dealer's plan, but not our's--not with a story like that to "tell around."

We proceeded to give him his "money's worth," without taking it from him. We made him promise, in the event that we suggested a cure, that he would never tell either a doctor, or a lawyer, since either or both might seek to prosecute us on the grounds of having violated the "medical practices act."

Then we told him seriously, that on Saturday nights before retiring, or on the night preceding a holiday, at which time he suspected the "witch" might cause him trouble, he should take an average-size waterglass, fill it to within an inch from the top with castor oil, retire and let the "old witch" do her damndest-- and to let nature take its course!

We suspected he was too old, or too lazy to get much exercise; that on Sundays and holidays he just loafed, failing to induce the proper action; thereupon we "sympathized and agreed" with him, and ordered the "prescription" accordingly!

Up to this time, years later, we have neither heard of a "witch murder" in the upper end of Dauphin county, nor have we thus far been prosecuted for our "violation" of the medical practices act. The "case" apparently was well "attended to."

> Doctors tell us the dosage was just about right!
>
> Lawyers just laugh about the matter!
>
> Judges, too, wink their eye, and laugh out aloud!
>
> Wherever we've told it, the public likes it . . .
>
> Yet, in spite of it's humor, it is all too true . . .

www.ingramcontent.com/pod-product-compliance
Lightning Source LLC
Chambersburg PA
CBHW040747020526
44118CB00040B/2702